A IS FOR...
ALCOHOLISM

ABORTION

ABUSE

ACCIDENTAL DEATH

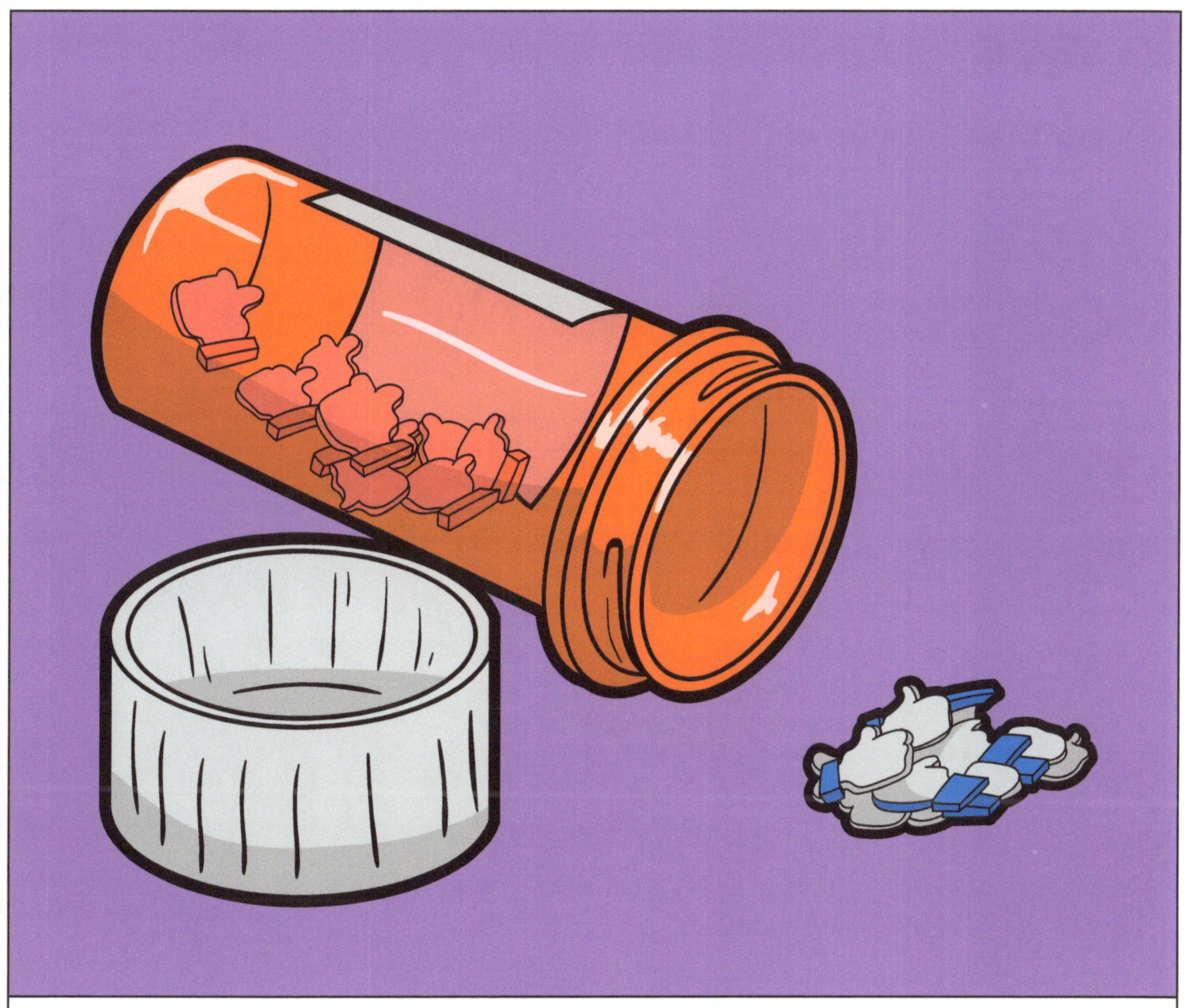

ADDICTION

ADULTERY

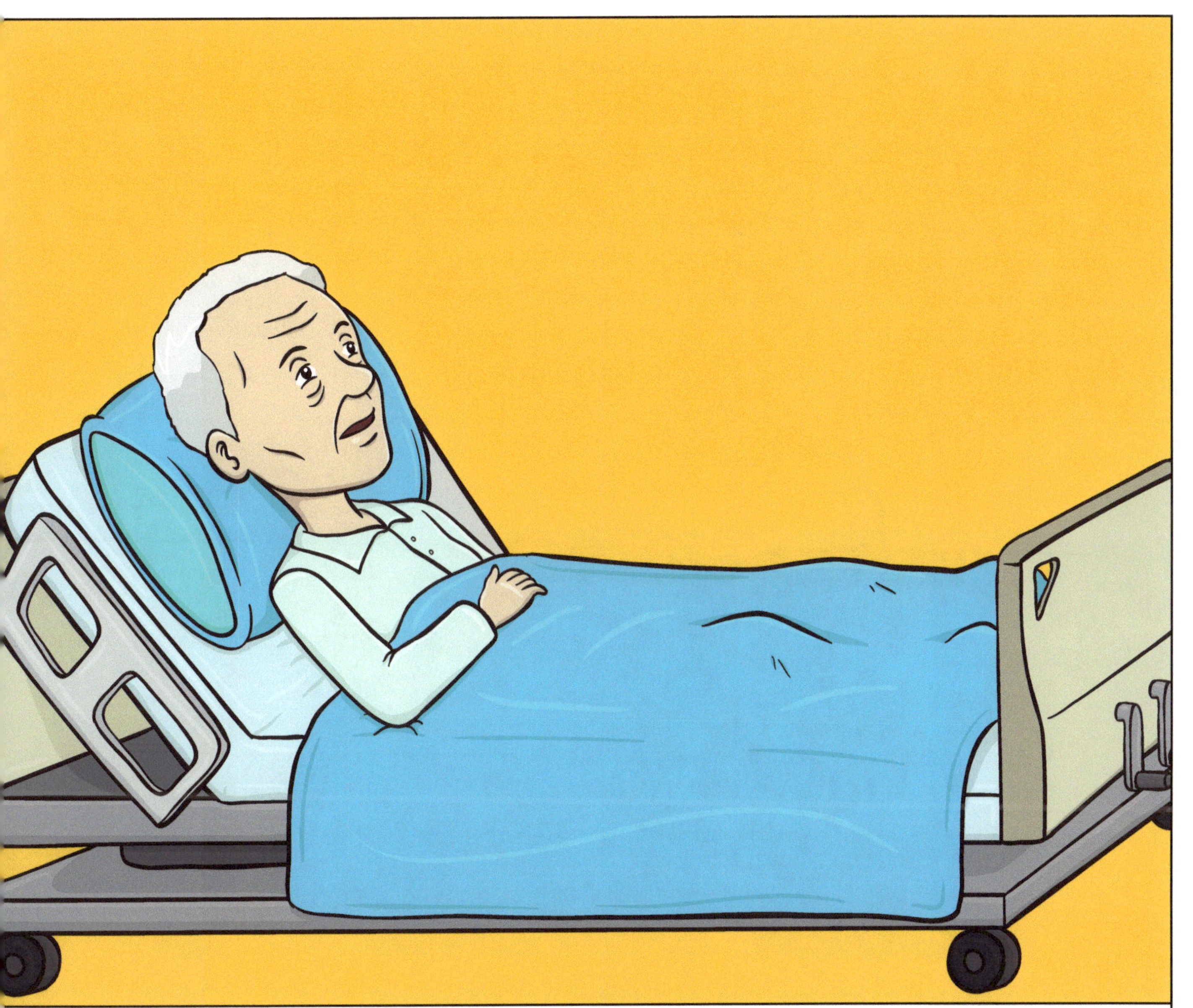

AFFLICTION

AFRAID

AIDS

AILMENT

AIRHEAD

AIRPLANE CRASH

ALCOHOLISM

ALIBI

ALIMONY

ALTERNATIVE LIFESTYLE

ALZHEIMER'S

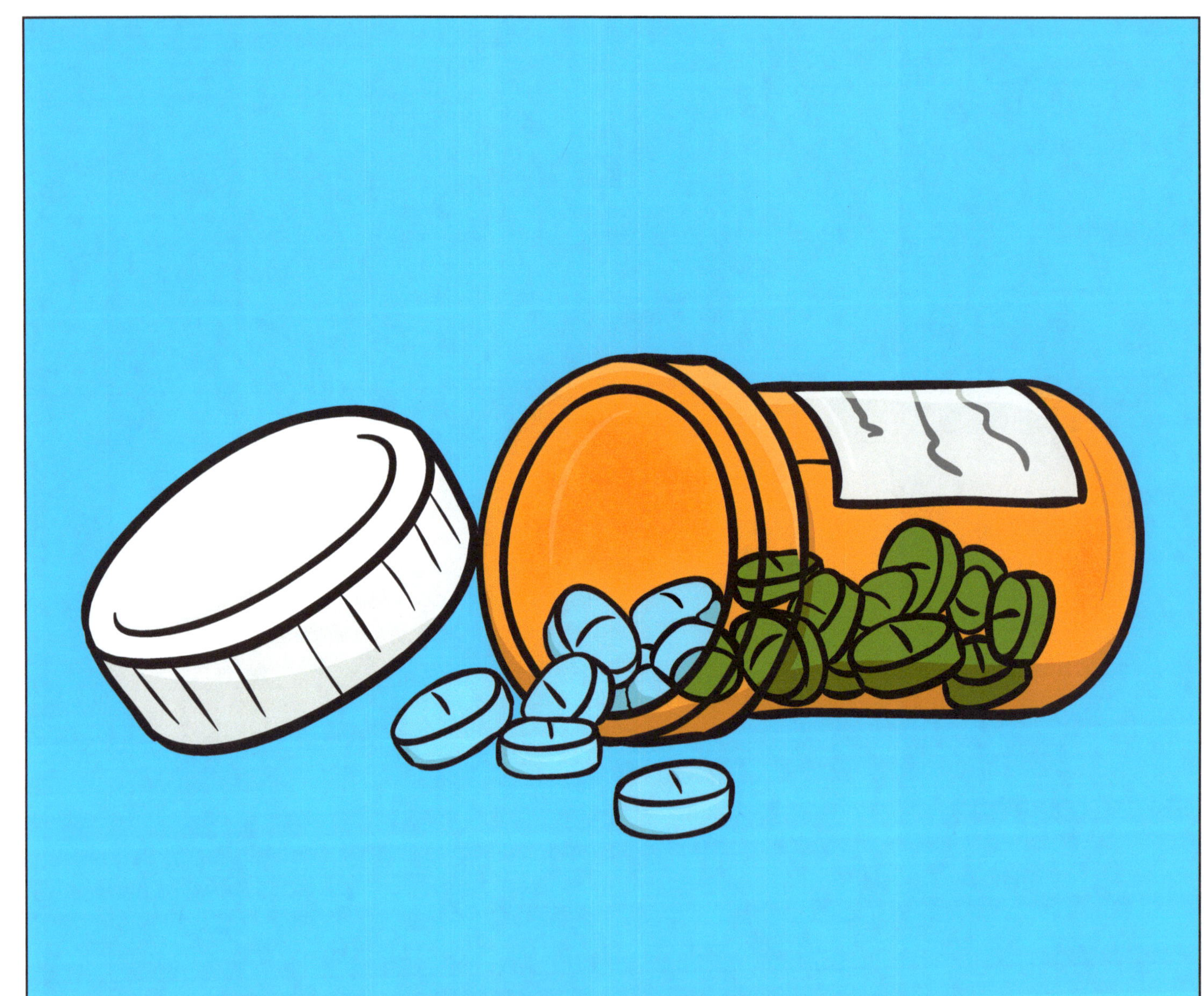

AMPHETAMINE

AMPUTATION

ANGER MANAGEMENT

ANUS

ANXIETY

ARGUMENT

ARRESTED

ARSON

ARYAN BROTHERHOOD

ASPHYXIATION

ATOMIC BOMB

ATTACKED

AXE

BAA BAA BLACK SHEEP
Deals With Another Routine Stop

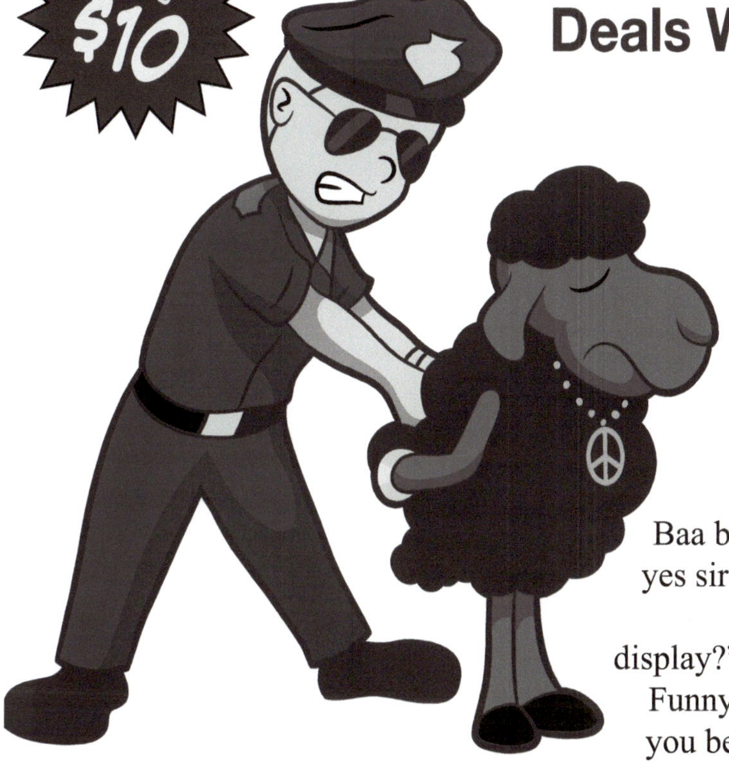

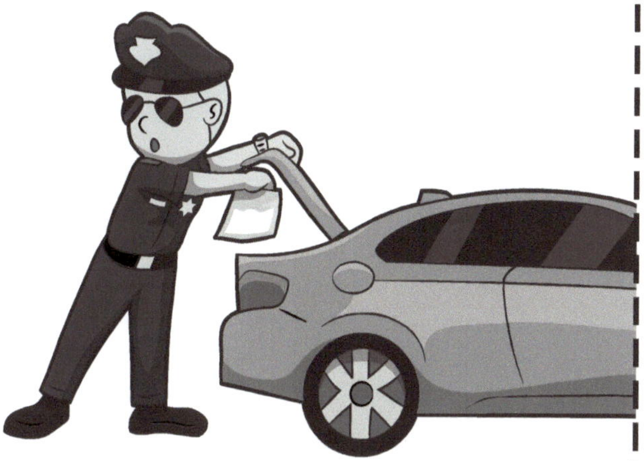

Baa baa black sheep please step out of the car. Yes sir yes sir please know I'm unarmed. Do you know why I stopped you today?. "Because of the fur color I display?". You match the description of a suspect I seek. Funny it's the 4th time to happen this week. I profiled you because you are black. And you drive a Mercedes which seems kinda whack.

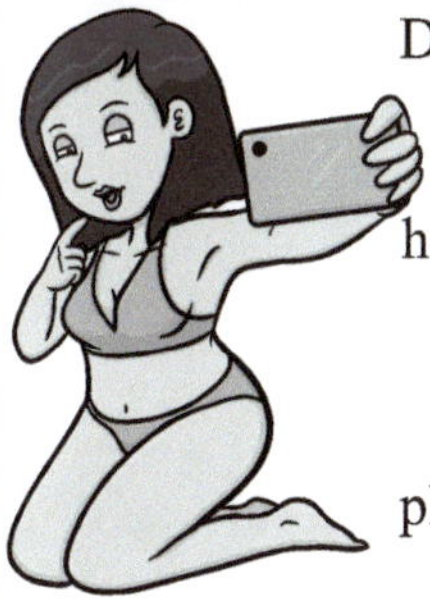

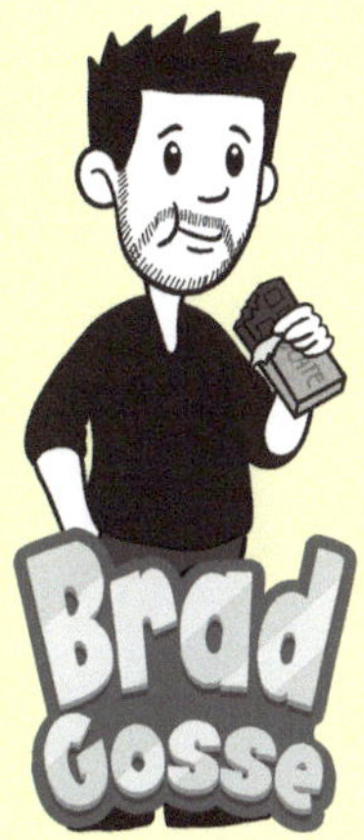

MOMMY GOT A DUI

Your mom has secrets. She hides her drinking from you… Until now. Mommy can't drive you to school and you're going to have to learn the bus routes.

INSOMNIAC & FRIENDS
The Clowns That Put You To Sleep

Yeetyeet likes to watch you sleep. Pickles under your bed he creeps. Switchblade eats your favorite stuffies. Pedo lures you away with puppies. Shifty plans to collect your teeth. Twisty smells your hair while you sleep. Clammy lives inside his van. Hank once had to kill a man. Tooty smells your dirty socks. Busby laughs at electric shocks. Twinkles spends the night robbing graves. Fappy keeps a few human slaves.

MY RACIST GRAN

WHY DADDY HITS MOMMY

A Kids Guide To Understanding Alcoholism

OK BOOMER

Boomer always complains at the store. But it was on sale yesterday!! When yesterday's special isn't available anymore. You shouldn't be such a slut. Boomer gives unsolicited advice. This smart phone is dumber than dirt. Boomer always struggles with his device. Boomer demands your supervisor.

CINNAMON

A horse forced into the sex trade.

DON'T BATHE WITH UNCLE JOE
Setting Boundaries With Adults

Uncle Joe lost his job. For misconduct in the workplace. He's coming to stay with us. You're going to have to learn to avoid his hands and more importantly. NEVER bathe with uncle Joe.

THIRST TRAPS
Why Moms Phone Keeps Blowing Up

DADDY'S A SIMP

Don't Expect Much Inheritance

MERCHANDISE
bradgosse.redbubble.com

BOOKS
amazon.com/author/bradgosse

www.ingramcontent.com/pod-product-compliance
Lightning Source LLC
Chambersburg PA
CBHW042003110726
48006CB00004B/969